GENERAL DIRECTIONS

All directions stated here are for all ornaments shown in this book. If procedures differ, it is so stated in the specific instructions for the ornament.

TRANSFERRING Patterns are transferred to the wood using carbon or transfer paper. I find it useful to first make a paper pattern on tracing paper so that you can easily see the imperfections in the wood when the pattern is placed on the wood. If, however, you are planning to make large quantities of an ornament, it is best to make a template. A template is made by cutting each pattern piece from 1/8" masonite. To transfer the design to the wood, draw around each pattern piece.

CUTTING OUT ORNAMENT In a process that I created to lower the cost of the wood, I cut all designs out of 1" pine. I then turn the piece on its side and slice the piece into 1/3rds or 1/4ths (depending how thick I wish the ornament to be). I end up with enough pieces to make 3 or 4 ornaments. With this process I not only drastically cut the cost of each ornament, but I can make different thicknesses for different parts of the ornament.

SANDING After all pattern pieces have been cut out, all surfaces and edges should be sanded using a fine grade of sandpaper. This is a very important step. It will set up the surface for painting. At this time the details of the ornament may be transferred onto the surface and used as a guide for painting.

   A second material used for sanding is a brown paper bag. This can be used interchangeably with the fine sandpaper when sanding in between coats of paint. It is less abrasive to the paint, and gives a wonderfully smooth finish.

BASECOATING All surfaces (front and back) receive two coats of paint with a thorough sanding in between each coat. Be sure to remove excess dust with a tack cloth before applying the second coat of paint.

DETAIL Most of the detail on each ornament is painted on with a fine brush at the time of painting. However, fine detail lines in black may be added *after* the ornament has been assembled and sprayed. I find that using an extra fine point permanent marker is wonderful.

PERSONALIZATION Whenever possible, try to personalize ornaments. This has always been a boost to my sales. I either paint the names on, if I know ahead who will receive it, or I use a permanent marker to add personalization at a moment's notice. (Great for craft shows!) I have included a simple alphabet on page 3, so practice a little and before you know it you will be ready to personalize. Should you make a mistake, do not despair! There are several products on the market that will easily remove the permanent marker without damaging the finish (see list of supplies).

ARTISTIC LICENSE It is important that you feel free to add your own special touches. For instance, if I have spattered a surface and you wish to leave it plain, feel free to. This is your project. The more that you gear the ornament to your painting expertise the more fun you will have.

PATTERN PIECES Within each ornament description the number of pattern pieces are given. The number and description pertains to the wooden pattern pieces only. Other items used, such as fabric, twine, etc., are not included in the number of pattern pieces listed.

SPATTER PAINTING To "spatter" an object, you should start with basecoating the item. When this is finished, you are ready to add the "texture" of spatter painting. Choose from a variety of tools: spatter brush (available in most craft stores), toothbrush, stencil brush, or stiff bristled paint brush. The choice is up to you!

   Load the brush with a color that will contrast with the base color of the object. It can be either a lighter or darker tone. Do not overload the brush with paint that is either too thick or too thin, but instead choose paint that is a workable consistency.

   Run a thumb across the bristles of the brush, allowing the droplets to "spatter" over the surface of the work. To add interest, more than one color may be spattered.

BLUSH The term "blush" merely designates a gentle treatment given to the cheeks of various ornaments. The desired effect of blushing is to add just a hint of color to the cheeks. Blush can be achieved in two ways:

   a. **Dry brush:** Load brush with desired blush color. Wipe excess paint off on a piece of paper towel until only a small amount remains. Gently dry brush this onto the cheeks.

b. **Diluted paint:** Select blush color and add water to make a translucent wash. Gently add this to the cheeks.

FLOAT For all of you that have never quite been able to conquer the technique of "floating" a color, have heart! I use a mock technique that is as effective, and very easy. It is also quite a bit easier to do this on the small surface of an ornament.

First, a color is chosen that is several shades darker than the base color. This color is then thinned with water (about 50/50). This "wash" is then painted wherever an accent color is desired. After it has dried, a very thin line of black may be applied over the accented area, or this can be done by using a fine permanent marker after the ornament has been sprayed. Note: It may be easier to add the black accent line (with a brush) before the ornament is assembled.

GENERAL SUPPLIES

WOOD All of my ornaments have been cut from 1" white pine. There are several grades of lumber ranging from #3 (the lowest grade with the most defects) to clear (the highest grade with few imperfections). The cost will be reflected in the grade that you buy. Since ornaments use small surfaces, you can usually get by with a lower grade of lumber, or even scraps. You can also use poplar (always clear grade) or either 1/8" or 1/4" masonite.

SPRAY FINISH An acrylic spray finish is preferable because of its compatibility with the paint. You may choose either a gloss finish, or a satin finish. Apply two coats of spray (front and back) to all ornaments.

SANDPAPER A "fine" grade of sandpaper or brown paper bag is used on all projects.

GLUE All projects are glued before they are sprayed. A good wood glue, such as Titebond II is excellent; however, superglue or a good household cement may be used. When gluing small pieces together it is advisable to use a toothpick to transfer the glue from the tube to the project piece.

Please note: Painted surfaces do *not* adhere permanently to one another. Therefore, when painting projects, leave a little section (where pieces are to be glued together) unpainted *or* put a piece of masking tape on that area and paint over the tape, which will be removed after paint has dried. And, if you forget to do either of the above, just sand a small area (where the pieces are to be glued) to rough up the surface which will create some "tooth" in order to get better adhesion.

BRUSHES Unless otherwise noted, a #7 round brush was used for all basecoating and a #0 round brush was used for all detail painting.

STRING Metallic thread of either silver or gold is used unless otherwise noted.

DETAIL PEN (optional) Sharpie extra fine point is applicable to all projects. If you choose to use another pen, be sure that it is permanent and will not wipe off of the sprayed surface.

PERMANENT PEN REMOVER (optional) A dried latex paint remover can be found at all hardware stores. It will remove the permanent marker without damaging the finish if the ornament has been sprayed and is thoroughly dry.

PAINT Acrylic paint is used on all projects. When trying to match either the brand names or the paint colors that have been used in these projects, do not be too concerned. Only you will know if you have chosen a comparable color. This is another area where your free will should reign! The colors listed in the following Conversion Chart are simply one possibility. Don't hesitate to use the colors that you already have on hand.

COLOR CONVERSIONS AMONG MAJOR PAINT BRANDS[1]

DecoArt Americana	Delta Ceramcoat	Plaid FolkArt
Antique Gold	Antique Gold	Harvest Gold
Blue Haze	Blue Spruce + Avalon Blue	Township Blue
Burnt Sienna	Burnt Sienna	Molasses
Cadmium Yellow	Yellow	School Bus Yellow
Country Red	Cardinal Red	Calico Red
Dark Chocolate	Burnt Umber	Chocolate Fudge
Dusty Rose	Normandy Rose	Berries n' Cream
Flesh Tone	Fleshtone	Skintone
Forest Green	Forest Green	Green Meadow
French Grey/Blue	Midnight Blue + White	Settler's Blue
Glorious Gold (Metallic)	Metallic Gold (Gleams)	Pure Gold (Metallic)
Gooseberry Pink + Tit. White	Gypsy Rose + White	Salmon + Tit. White
Grey Sky	Bridgeport + White	Dove Gray
Holly Green	Green Isle	Evergreen
Lamp Black[2]	Black	Licorice
Mauve	Rose Mist	Potpourri Rose
Navy Blue	Prussian Blue	Thunder Blue + Blue Ribbon
Sable Brown	Toffee	Honeycomb
Sand	Ivory	Taffy
Titanium White[3]	White	Titanium White
True Blue	Pthalo Blue	True Blue
True Red	Fire Red	Cardinal Red
Warm Neutral	Wild Rice	Milkshake

Notes: 1. Converson colors are similar, but not exact matches; 2. previously Ebony Black; 3. previously Snow White

Practice Alphabet

Aa Bb Cc Dd Ee Ff Gg

Hh Ii Jj Kk Ll Mm

Nn Oo Pp Qq Rr Ss

Tt Uu Vv Ww Xx Yy Zz

1. GINGERBREAD BOY WITH JOY (Photo on p. 7)

3 Pattern Pieces: 1 JOY, 1 gingerbread boy upper body, 1 gingerbread boy legs

PALETTE
CR Country Red
FG Forest Green
GW Gooseberry Pink + White
LB Lamp Black
SB Sable Brown
TR True Red
TW Titanium White

ADDITIONAL SUPPLIES
1/8" red ribbon (3" piece for each ornament)

PRELIMINARY PAINTING
Follow the General Directions for transferring, cutting, and basecoating. Use TR to basecoat JOY, and SB to basecoat the gingerbread boy pieces.

DETAILING
A simple plaid design (see Worksheet #2, page 9) in TW is placed on top of the spattered JOY. Paint "pollywog" leaves with FG, berries with CR (see Worksheet #1, page 8). The Gingerbread Boy is detailed by painting "icing" lines with TW; eyes, nose, and mouth with LB; and cheeks with GW.

FINISHING
Glue all the pieces together and spray. Drill a 1/16" hole in completed ornament and thread with metallic thread for hanging.

2. SANTA WITH STOCKINGS (Photo on p. 7)

5 Pattern Pieces: 1 Santa; 4 stockings (of course, you can adjust the number of stockings to your own family)

PALETTE
AG Antique Gold
CR Country Red
DR Dusty Rose
FB French Grey/Blue
FG Forest Green
FT Flesh Tone
GS Grey Sky
LB Lamp Black
TW Titanium White
WN Warm Neutral

PRELIMINARY PAINTING
Follow the General Directions for transferring, cutting, and basecoating. Use CR to basecoat Santa's hat and coat. Use FG for his mittens, and TW to cover hat brim, face, and beard/mustache on the first coat. On the second coat, use TW for the hat, brim and beard/mustache, but use FT for the face. Another coat of FT may be necessary. Each stocking is basecoated a different color. My choices were FB, CR (lightened with TW), FG (lightened with TW) and AG.

DETAILING

Detail is added by first spatter painting Santa's coat with WN. Be sure to immediately wipe extra off of hat brim, face, beard, and mittens. You may opt to spatter paint coat and hat *before* you basecoat the hat brim, face, and beard. Add simple plaid (see Worksheet #2, page 9) to coat and hat with WN. On face, paint in cheeks with DR. Float hat brim, mustache, and beard with GS. Lighten CR with TW and paint on nose and bottom lip. Add eyebrows in TW, "pollywog" leaves with FG, and berries in CR (see Worksheet #1, page 8). The final detail for the face is very thin lines in LB around hat, beard, and mustache. Fill in mouth and eyes with LB. Outline each stocking with a darker version of the basecoat color.

FINISHING

Glue all pieces together and spray. Drill a 1/16" hole and string with metallic thread for hanging.

3. BIRD HOUSE WITH TIN ROOF (Photo on p. 7)

3 Pattern Pieces: 1 back arch, 1 birdhouse, 1 bird; tin roof is separate

PALETTE

CR Country Red
FG Forest Green
LB Lamp Black
TW Titanium White
WN Warm Neutral

ADDITIONAL SUPPLIES

Tin for roof (1 1/8" x 3 1/2" per ornament)
Hot glue
Dowel rod (1/8" x 3/4" per ornament)
Spanish moss

PRELIMINARY PAINTING

Follow the General Directions for transferring, cutting, and basecoating. Use WN to basecoat the back arch. Use FG to basecoat the birdhouse, after the dowel rod "perch" has been added and hole drilled for birdhouse opening. Use CR to basecoat the bird.

DETAILING

Add detail by painting pollywog leaves (see Worksheet #1, page 8) at top and bottom of arch using FG. The pollywog leaves on the birdhouse and bird are FG lightened with TW, and the heart is painted with CR. Add roses (see Worksheet #1, page 8) to top and bottom of arch. Outline the bird and wing with LB; add eye and beak in the same color. Finally add dots of CR over the pollywog leaves and at the bird's neck.

FINISHING

Assemble ornament by gluing birdhouse to back arch. Do not glue on the bird at this time. Spray all pieces, and glue tin roof on. Glue small amount of Spanish moss in the hole to look like a nest. Glue bird onto perch. Drill a 1/16" hole in the top, and string with metallic thread for hanging.

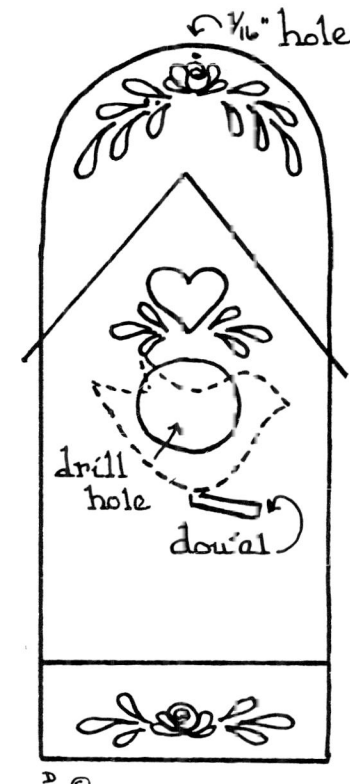

4. CAROLING BEAR (Photo at right)

2 Pattern Pieces: 1 body and head (with hat), 1 pair of arms and music book

PALETTE
CR Country Red
FG Forest Green
LB Lamp Black
SB Sable Brown
TR True Red
TW Titanium White
WN Warm Neutral

PRELIMINARY PAINTING
Follow the General Directions for transferring, cutting, and basecoating. Start by painting the body and face of the bear with SB. Basecoat the hat and sweater TR and the music book, hat brim, and pompom with TW.

DETAILING
Add detail by painting paws in SB on top of the music book, and outline the music book with a band of FG. Paint a "snout" circle on the bear's face with WN. When this is dry, use LB to add eyes, nose, and mouth. Mix SB and WN to use as a fine line detail on the ear, legs, and feet. CR is used in the same fashion to detail the hat and sweater. Add holly leaves of FG and dots of CR, and the ornament is ready for finishing.

FINISHING
Glue pieces together and spray. Drill a 1/16" hole in the top of the hat brim. String with metallic thread for hanging.

5. ANGEL WITH RAFFIA WINGS (Photo at right; pattern on p. 11)

4 Pattern Pieces: 1 angel, 3 stars

PALETTE
AG Antique Gold
DR Dusty Rose
FG Forest Green
FT Flesh Tone
LB Lamp Black
SB Sable Brown
TW Titanium White

ADDITIONAL SUPPLIES
Eight 18" long raffia strands per ornament
26 gauge wire (9" long)
Hot glue

PRELIMINARY PAINTING
Follow the General Directions for transferring, cutting, and basecoating. Use FT to basecoat entire head (hair section included) and hands. Basecoat dress with FG. Paint a second coat of FT on head and hands and allow to dry. Basecoat stars and paint in hair color with AG.

DETAILING
Stipple the dress (see Worksheet #1, page 8) with a mixture of FG and TW. When that has dried use an even lighter mix of FG and TW to add details to the neck, sleeves, and hem of dress. Dots of TW are then placed at the bottom of dress. Edge the hair with a mixture of AG and SB; add a FG bow to act as a halo. Add eyes, nose, and mouth with LB, and blush (see description on page 1) on cheeks with DR. At this time you should not assemble ornament, but go to the finishing stage.

FINISHING
Spray all pieces. Drill a 1/16" hole in the top of each star, in each hand, and in the top of the angel. Place wire through each star giving a twist to assure that the star stays in place. Thread wire through hands to secure and wrap the ends around a small dowel rod to form a spiral shape. Then remove the dowel. String the ornament with metallic thread. Tie the raffia strands in a bow leaving tails of about 3 1/2". Trim. Hot glue the raffia wings in place.

#1, p. 4
#2, p. 4
#3, p. 5
#4, p. 6
#5, p. 6

Worksheet #1

Pollywog Leaves

load brush and flatten it against work. Lift and pull to attain a "tail".

Holly Leaves

Berries
1. basecoat
2. Lighten basecoat and add an accent
3. Accent with white
4. Add black dot
5. Optional: outline

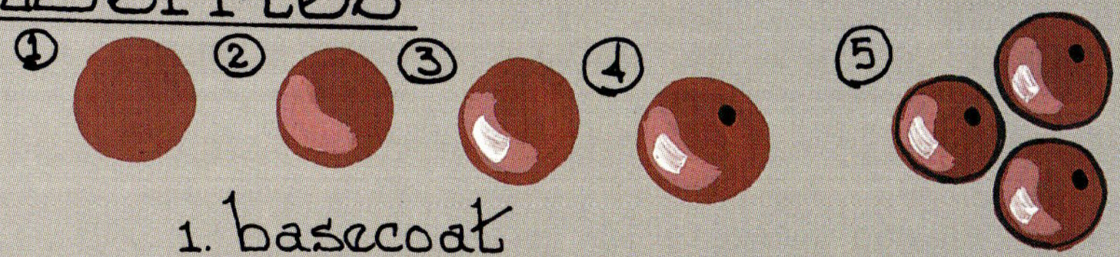

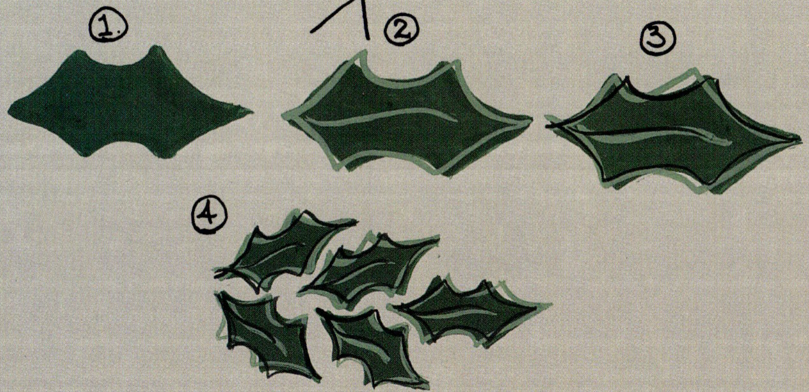

1. Basecoat holly leaf
2. Outline and paint with lightened basecoat.
3. Outline again with Black
* When outlining be careful! Do not stay exactly on basecoated leaf.
4. Group leaves on larger spaces.

Roses
1. Paint base paint oval
2. Lighten base paint and paint pollywogs
3. Add 2 more pollywogs.
4. Dot with white
5. Add white pollywog accents
6. Add stems and leaves

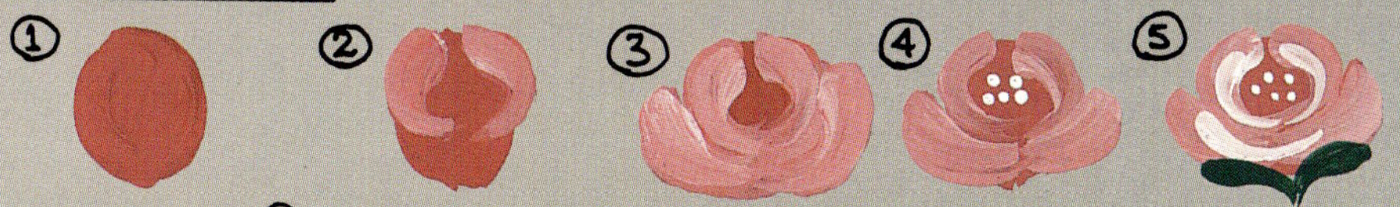

Stipple
1. Basecoat in choice of colors
2. Lighten basecoat with white and "dab" on paint using a stencil brush.
3. Optional: "dab" a second color over the top. (i.e. Black)

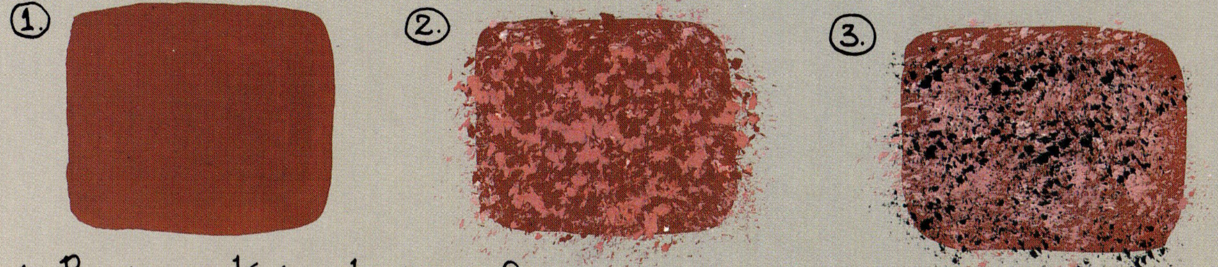

Worksheet #2

Simple Plaid (figures 1 and 2)

① ②

1 and 2. Basecoat in choice of color. Draw either single (1) or double (2) lines in a contrasting color going vertically and horizontally.

Double Plaid (3)

3. Complete all stages of figures 1 and 2, then change to a second contrasting color and add another set of lines.

Patchwork

①

1. Basecoat and divide area into irregular shapes.

②

2. In each area paint a "simple plaid" with a variety of colors.

③

3. Now "double plaid" the areas; antique the entire space and finish with black "stitch" lines.

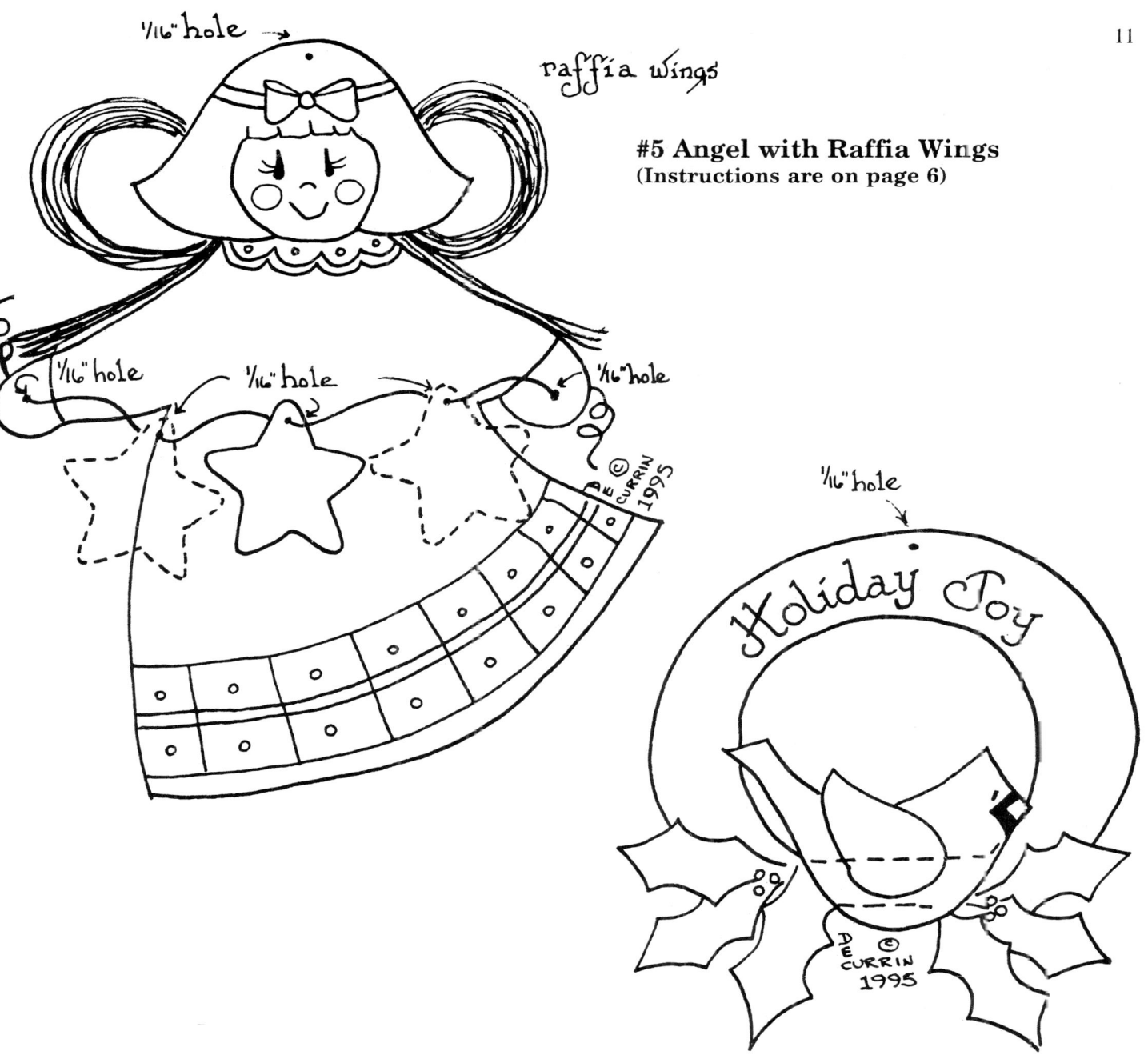

#5 Angel with Raffia Wings
(Instructions are on page 6)

6. CARDINAL HOLIDAY JOY (Photo at left)

2 Pattern Pieces: 1 bird, 1 arch with holly

PALETTE
TR True Red
FG Forest Green
WN Warm Neutral
LB Lamp Black
CR Country Red

PRELIMINARY PAINTING
Follow the General Directions for transferring, cutting, and base-coating. Use WN to basecoat the arch; FG to basecoat the holly leaves, and TR to basecoat the cardinal.

DETAILING
Using TR paint a "stitching" line across top and bottom of the arch. Write the words "Holiday Joy" with FG. (This space could also be left blank for future personalizing.) Detail the leaves with a fine line of LE, and add berry dots of TR. The cardinal is first outlined with a float of CR, and then a very fine line of LB is added on top. Beak and eye are LB.

FINISHING
Glue both ornament pieces together, and spray. Drill a 1/16" hole in the top and thread with metallic thread for hanging.

7. TRIANGLE NATIVITY (Photo on p. 10; pattern at right)

4 Pattern Pieces: 1 star, 1 triangle with baby in crèche, 1 Mary, 1 Joseph

PALETTE
AG Antique Gold
CR Country Red
DR Dusty Rose
FB French Grey/Blue
FG Forest Green
FT Flesh Tone
LB Lamp Black
M   Mauve
NB Navy Blue
S   Sand
SB Sable Brown
TW Titanium White

PRELIMINARY PAINTING
Follow the General Directions for transferring, cutting, and basecoating. Use NB to basecoat the triangle; FB to basecoat the robe of Joseph, and M to basecoat the robe of Mary. All faces are basecoated with FT. The baby's wrap is painted a mixture of FG and TW. The crèche is painted SB, and the star is painted AG.

DETAILING
Both Mary's and Joseph's robes are detailed with a darker version of their basecoat (for Joseph mix FB and NB; for Mary mix M and CR). Detail the baby's wrap with FG. Add Straw by lightly brushing S down from the baby. S is also used to add pollywog details to the star and down the sides and bottom of the triangle. Eyes and mouths are detailed in LB, and cheeks are added with DR.

FINISHING
Glue all pieces together and spray. Drill a 1/16" hole in the top of the star, and string with metallic thread for hanging.

8. SANTA AND RUDOLPH (Photo on p. 10)

2 Pattern Pieces: 1 Santa, 1 Rudolph

PALETTE
CR Country Red
DC Dark Chocolate
DR Dusty Rose
FG Forest Green
FT Flesh Tone
GS Grey Sky
LB Lamp Black
SB Sable Brown
TR True Red
TW Titanium White
WN Warm Neutral

ADDITIONAL SUPPLIES
Fabric (6" square per ornament for Santa's sack)
Cotton ball or tissue for stuffing the fabric bag
Twine (18" piece folded in half per ornament)

PRELIMINARY PAINTING
Follow the General Directions for transferring, cutting, and basecoating. Start by painting Santa's hat and body with TR; boots with LB; and hat brim, pompom, face, and beard with TW. Rudolph is painted SB with WN antlers. Face is painted FT on the second coat.

DETAILING
Hat and body are outlined with CR; cheeks are added with DR, eyebrows with TW, and mustache/beard are outlined with GS. You can make the surface look fuzzy by dabbing brush in TW and GS, and tapping it on the hat brim and pompom. That same technique is used with SB and DC for texturing Rudolph's body. Use TW, then LB, for Rudolph's eyes. His ears and eyebrows are added with a mixture of SB and DC. Leaves of FG are added to both Santa's hat brim and Rudolph's neck; topped off with CR dots. Lighten CR

with TW to make Santa's nose and lower lip, then fill in mouth and eyes with LB. Paint a LB mouth on Rudolph, and we can't forget a nose of CR! The final detail is added with a fine line around Santa's pompom, hat, hat brim, beard, mustache, and body.

FINISHING
Glue Santa and Rudolph together and spray. Make a sack by placing tissue in the center of the fabric square and gathering it up. Secure the top by tying twine in a tight bow. Trim off excess fabric, and glue sack to Santa's front. Drill a 1/16" hole in the right side of the hat brim and thread with metallic thread for hanging.

9. ANGEL WITH TREE, HEART, AND STAR (Photo on p. 10)

8 Pattern Pieces: 1 body, 2 arms, 2 wings, 1 star, 1 heart, 1 tree

PALETTE
AG   Antique Gold
CR   Country Red
DR   Dusty Rose
FG   Forest Green
FT   Flesh Tone
LB   Lamp Black
SB   Sable Brown
TW   Titanium White
WN   Warm Neutral

ADDITIONAL SUPPLIES
26 gauge wire (7" piece per ornament)

PRELIMINARY PAINTING
Follow the General Directions for transferring, cutting, and base coating. Start by painting the body and arms with CR, and the face (including the hair area), hands, and feet FT. The wings are WN. The tree is FG with a SB trunk; the star is AG; and the heart is CR. On the second coat of basecoating, the face is painted FT, and the hair is painted AG.

DETAILING
A double plaid (see Worksheet #2, page 9) is painted on the dress and arms using FG and TW. (Because I like the finished look, I always continue the design on the back.) Outline the wings with a lightened mix of WN and TW. Also spatter the dress, arms, and wings with this same mix. When you spatter be sure to wipe the excess off of the face, hands, and feet. To detail the tree, star, and heart merely lighten the basecoat color with TW and outline each shape. Pollywog leaves in FG and berries in CR are painted over the hair (see Worksheet #1, page 8). The face is completed by painting eyes, nose, and mouth with LB, and cheeks with DR. A very fine line of LB around each shape on the wire will complete the detailing.

FINISHING
Glue arms and wings in place and spray. Drill a 1/16' hole in the top of the tree, star, heart, hands, and back wing. Thread the wire through the tree, star, and heart then twist the wire to hold each shape in place. Thread wire through hands, and secure by wrapping ends around a small dowel rod forming a spiral shape. Then remove the dowel. String with metallic thread for hanging.

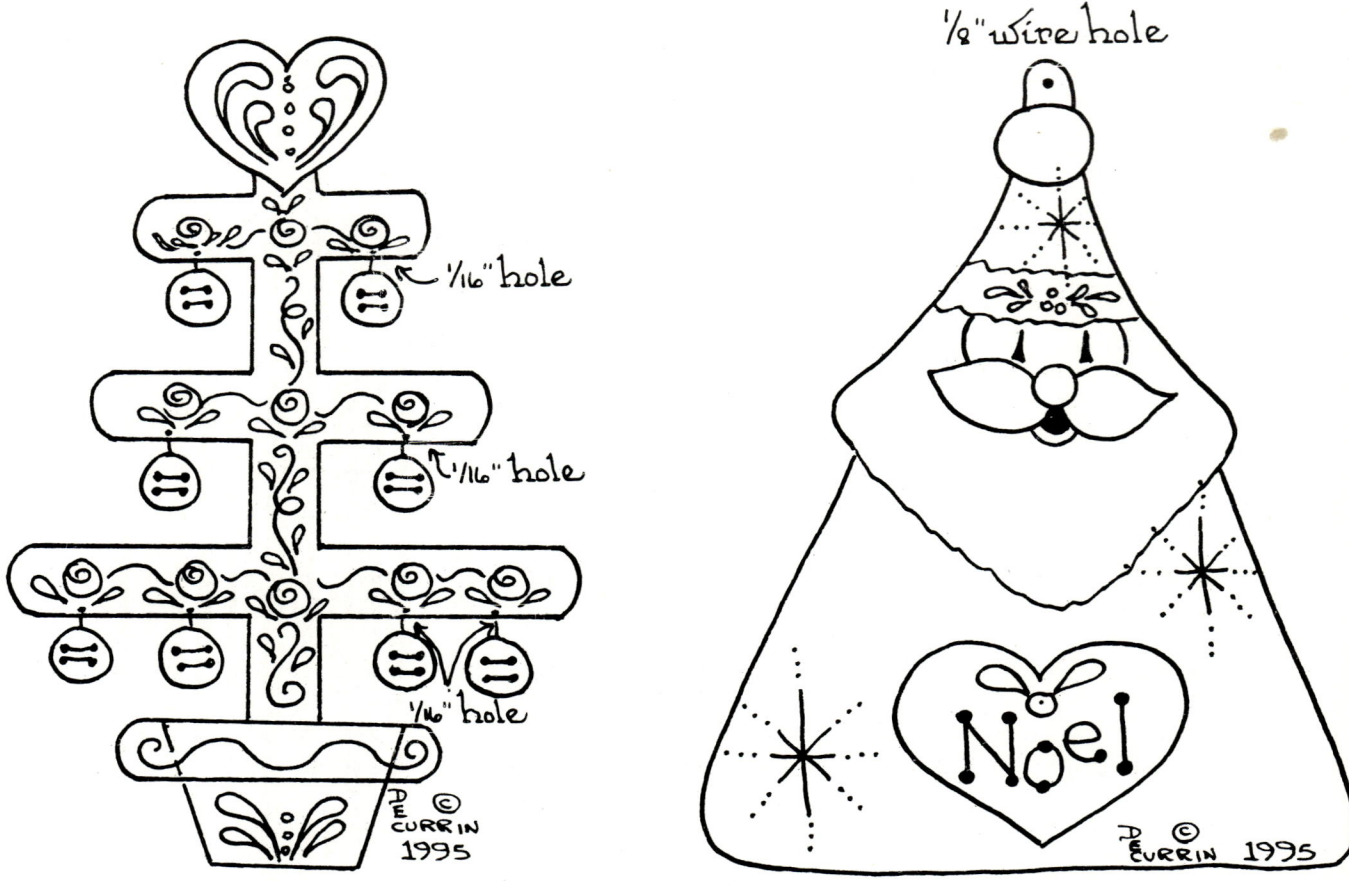

10. BELL TREE (Photo on p. 10)

2 Pattern Pieces: 1 tree with base and 1 base topper

PALETTE
CR Country Red
FG Forest Green
TW Titanium White

ADDITIONAL SUPPLIES
26 gauge wire
Mini jingle bells (eight per ornament)

PRELIMINARY PAINTING
Follow the General Directions for transferring, cutting, and basecoating. Start by painting the heart and base pieces CR. Paint the tree FG.

DETAILING
CR and FG are both lightened with TW to add the detail. Add designs to the heart and the base pieces. Roses (see Worksheet #1, page 8) are painted with the lightened CR. Add leaves and detail with lightened FG.

FINISHING
Glue the base accent on and spray. Drill 1/16" holes as indicated on pattern for the bells, and also at the top for thread. Wire bells in place and finish by stringing with metallic thread for hanging.

11. TRIANGLE SANTA (Photo on p. 16)

2 Pattern Pieces: 1 body and 1 heart

PALETTE
CR Country Red
DR Dusty Rose
FG Forest Green
FT Flesh Tone
GS Grey Sky
LB Lamp Black
TW Titanium White

ADDITIONAL SUPPLIES
Twine (three 18" strands per ornament)
19 gauge wire

PRELIMINARY PAINTING
Follow the General Directions for transferring, cutting, and basecoating. Start by painting the hat and body FG. The pompom and face are painted TW on the first coat, and then the face is painted FT on the second coat. The heart is painted CR.

DETAILING
Spatter the hat and body first with LB, then TW. Be sure to wipe excess off of face and pompom. See Santa Face #3 on Worksheet #4, page 25. Use DR for the cheeks; LB for the eyes and open mouth; GS and TW for the beard and mustache, and lightened CR for the nose and lower lip. Snowflakes and hat brim are painted in TW; pollywog leaves in FG; and berries in CR (see Worksheet #2, page 9). Spatter heart with LB.

FINISHING
Glue on the heart and spray. Drill a 1/8" hole for the wire. Use twine to tie a bow around the wire.

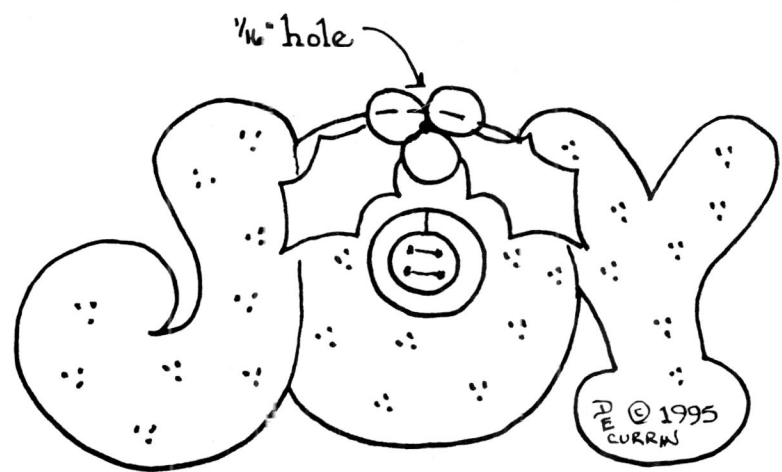

12. JOY (Photo on p. 16)

2 Pattern Pieces: 1 JOY and 1 holly/berries

PALETTE
CR Country Red
HG Holly Green
LB Lamp Black
TR True Red
TW Titanium White

ADDITIONAL SUPPLIES
26 gauge wire
1 mini jingle bell per ornament

PRELIMINARY PAINTING
Follow the General Directions for transferring, cutting, and basecoating. Paint the "Joy" TW, the holly leaves HG, and the berries TR.

DETAILING
Outline the word "JOY" with TR and add dots of the same color. (See Worksheet #1, page 8 for instructions on detailing the holly leaves and berries.)

FINISHING
Glue pieces together and spray. Drill a 1/16" hole in the top of the berries, and also at the top inside of the "O." String the bell inside the "O" with wire. String the ornament with metallic thread for hanging.

#11, p. 15

#13, p. 18

#12, p. 15

#15, p. 19

#14, p. 18

13. FAMILY IN BED (Photo on p. 16)

9 Pattern Pieces: 1 bed, 4 heads, and 4 stockings

PALETTE
AG Antique Gold
DC Dark Chocolate
DR Dusty Rose
FT Flesh Tone
HG Holly Green
LB Lamp Black
SB Sable Brown
TB True Blue
TR True Red
TW Titanium White

PRELIMINARY PAINTING
Follow the General Directions for transferring, cutting, and basecoating. Start by painting the bed SB, the blanket TR; and the sheet and pillow TW. All faces are painted FT, and the hats and stockings are painted one each of TB, TR, HG, and AG. (Feel free to substitute other colors, especially if you know the sexes of the children.)

DETAILING
Paint a simple plaid (see Worksheet #2, page 9) on the blanket with HG. Also outline the sheet top and pillow in this color. Mix a small amount of DC with SB and detail the bed posts. Faces are detailed by painting eyes, noses, and mouths with LB; paint cheeks with DR. I chose to add names with TW to personalize the stockings, but you may wish to leave them blank to be personalized later.

FINISHING
Glue heads and stockings onto bed being sure to match hat and stocking color; spray. Drill a 1/16" hole in the top and string with metallic thread for hanging.

14. "HAPPY HOLLY DAYS" RECTANGLE (Photo on p. 16)

3 Pattern Pieces: 1 rectangle, 1 snowman and hat top, 1 hat brim

PALETTE
BS Burnt Sienna
CR Country Red
DC Dark Chocolate
FG Forest Green
LB Lamp Black
TW Titanium White

ADDITIONAL SUPPLIES
26 gauge wire (6")
Raffia (10" strands)
Fabric for scarf (4" x 1/2" per ornament)

PRELIMINARY PAINTING
Follow the General Directions for transferring, cutting, and basecoating. Start by staining the rectangle with a thinned mixture of DC and water. When that has thoroughly dried, dab on top with thinned TW (a damp paper towel dipped in TW). Paint snowman from hat on down with a mixture of TW and a very small amount of DC. The hat and brim are painted LB.

DETAILING
Paint holly leaves in FG then add a CR berry (see Worksheet #1, page 8). Sand snowman to give him a worn look, and add cheeks with a mixture of TW and BS. Nose is BS; eyes and mouth are LB. Paint the words "Happy Holly Days" in TW on rectangle. Spatter hat with TW.

FINISHING
Tie fabric around snowman's neck to form a scarf. Glue snowman on rectangle and, because this ornament has a rougher look than the others, do not spray it. Drill a 1/16" hole on either side at the top and thread the wire through, being sure to secure it with several twists. Tie raffia around wire on left side.

15. SANTA WITH BANNER (Photo on p. 16)

2 Pattern Pieces: 1 upper body and banner, 1 pair legs

PALETTE
DR Dusty Rose
FG Forest Green
FT Flesh Tone
GS Grey Sky
LB Lamp Black
TR True Red
TW Titanium White

PRELIMINARY PAINTING
Follow the General Directions for transferring, cutting, and basecoating. Start by painting the pants, hat, and coat with TR. The pompom, face/beard section, and cuffs are painted TW. The banner is painted FG, and the mittens are painted a lightened FG. Boots are painted LB.

DETAILING
Add the face by using FT, being careful to keep the shape of the hair and mustache. Outline the hat brim, pompom, and cuffs with GS. To detail the face, add cheeks of DR; mouth and eyes of LB. Use a mixture of DR and TR for the nose (see Worksheet #3, page 24). The banner is given a "stitch" line of TW with the words "Holiday Joy" also in TW.

FINISHING
Glue the two pieces together and spray. Drill a 1/16" hole in the hat and string with metallic thread for hanging.

16. SANTA WITH LIST (Photo on p. 17)

3 Pattern Pieces: 1 Santa body, 1 arm, 1 list

PALETTE
CY Cadmium Yellow
DR Dusty Rose
FG Forest Green
FT Flesh Tone
GG Glorious Gold
GS Grey Sky
LB Lamp Black
TR True Red
TW Titanium White

ADDITIONAL SUPPLIES
Cotton batting for beard
1/2 toothpick per ornament (for pencil)
Hot glue

PRELIMINARY PAINTING
Follow the General Directions for transferring, cutting, and base coating. Start by painting the arm and body TR. Paint the head FT, the boots LB, and the mitten FG. Paint the list TW and the pencil CY. The pencil's eraser is a mixture of DR and TR; the tip is LB.

DETAILING
To detail the face paint eyes and mouth LB, cheeks DR, eyebrows TW, and nose a mixture of DR and TR. Last of all, add the glasses in GG. Use a lightened mixture of FG and TW to detail the mittens with a simple plaid (see Worksheet #2, page 9). The list is easily finished with a fine outline of GS. I find it is best to wait to add the words "Santa's List" until after the ornament has been sprayed. At that time you may use a permanent marker.

FINISHING
Drill a small hole in the side of head in which to insert the pencil. Be sure to add a drop of glue to the pencil for safe measure! Hot glue the batting onto the face by placing the glue at the back of the head. Glue arm and list on top of the beard. Drill a 1/16" hole in top of head and string with metallic thread for hanging.

17. RUDOLPH WITH CANDY (Photo on p. 17)

2 Pattern Pieces: 1 body with antlers, 1 candy box with candy canes

PALETTE
DC Dark Chocolate
HG Holly Green
LB Lamp Black
SB Sable Brown
TR True Red
TW Titanium White
WN Warm Neutral

PRELIMINARY PAINTING
Follow the General Directions for transferring, cutting, and basecoating. Start by painting the body and head SB, the antlers and tail WN, the candy canes TW, and the candy box HG.

DETAILING
The most important thing to do first is to define the face and body by outlining them with a mixture of SB and DC. The ears and eyebrows can also be added at this time. Eyes are painted on with TW first and then LB. "Candy stripe" the candy canes with TR, and using the same color, add Rudolph's identifying mark—his red nose! To complete the detailing, write "Santa's Candy" on the candy box, and run a thin line of TW down the middle of each candy cane.

FINISHING
Glue the two pieces together and spray. Drill a 1/16" hole in the top of the antlers and string with metallic thread for hanging.

18. UPSIDE DOWN ANGEL (Photo on p. 17)

3 Pattern Pieces: 1 body and arms; 1 head, wings, and collar; 1 star

PALETTE
AG Antique Gold
CR Country Red
DR Dusty Rose
FG Forest Green
FT Flesh Tone
LB Lamp Black
SB Sable Brown
TW Titanium White
WN Warm Neutral

PRELIMINARY PAINTING
Follow the General Directions for transferring, cutting, and basecoating. Start by painting the dress and arms FG, making sure to leave room for the band of WN at the hem. Paint the entire head/wing/collar piece a mixture of TW and WN. The star can be painted AG; the hands and feet FT.

DETAILING
Paint in the face with FT, and the hair with AG. Outline the hair with a mixture of AG and SB. The eyes, nose, and mouth are LB; the cheeks DR (see Worksheet #3, page 24). Detailing the collar and wings is easy with a thin line of FG and two CR hearts. The same CR hearts are painted at the hem of the dress; add FG leaves. Add a simple plaid (see Worksheet #2, page 9) on the dress and arms in WN and the angel is ready for finishing.

FINISHING
Glue all pieces together and spray. Drill two 1/16" holes in the feet and string with metallic thread for hanging.

19. SNOWMAN FAMILY (Photo on p. 17)

9 Pattern Pieces: 4 snowmen and hat tops, 4 hat brims, 1 heart

PALETTE
BS Burnt Sienna
CR Country Red
DC Dark Chocolate
LB Lamp Black
TW Titanium White

ADDITIONAL SUPPLIES
26 gauge wire (7" piece for each ornament)
Twine (two 7" pieces per ornament)
Fabric scraps for scarves (4" x 1/2" per ornament)
Hot glue

PRELIMINARY PAINTING
Follow the General Directions for transferring, cutting, and basecoating. Start by lightly penciling in a line to separate the hat from the snowman's face. Now basecoat the hats of the father and two children in LB. The brims are painted to match. Mother's hat and brim are painted in CR. If you want to make the snow children look more like girls, paint their hats and brims in CR instead of LB. Paint the front of all the snowmen with a mixture of TW and a very small amount of DC. Paint the heart with CR, and after this has dried, sand all pieces to make them look old. Stain all pieces front and back with a thin mixture of water and DC.

DETAILING
Glue on the hat brims, then spatter paint all of the snowmen and heart with TW. Add the details of their faces by painting cheeks with a very light mixture of BS and TW, eyes and mouths with LB, and noses with BS (except Mother who has a LB nose).

FINISHING
This is another ornament that looks better unsprayed because of the worn look. Tie the fabric scraps around the necks of the snowmen, and hold ends down with a small dab of hot glue. With hot glue assemble the ornament by gluing the heart between the parents, and adding the children on either side of the heart. Drill a 1/16" hole on each parent's hat brim and thread the wire through. Be sure to give the wire a good twist to secure it. Finish by tying the twine at one end of the wire.

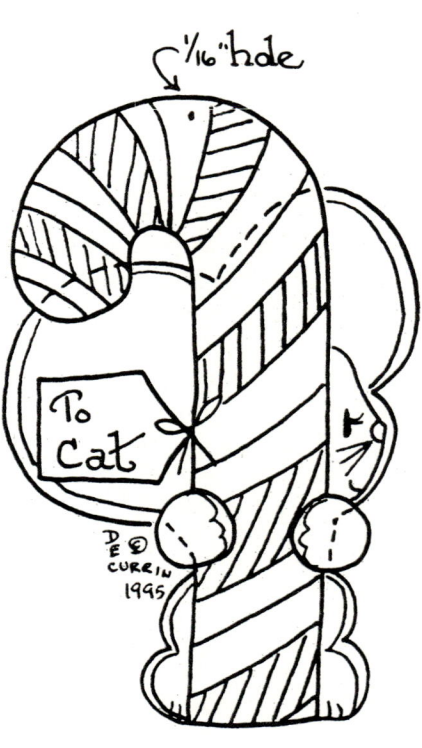

20. MOUSE WITH CANDY CANE (Photo on p. 17)

3 Pattern Pieces: 1 mouse body, 1 candy cane, 1 tag

PALETTE
GS Grey Sky
LB Lamp Black
TR True Red
TW Titanium White

ADDITIONAL SUPPLIES
1/8" green ribbon (4" piece per ornament)

PRELIMINARY PAINTING
Follow the General Directions for transferring, cutting, and basecoating. Start by painting the mouse's body GS. Paint the candy cane, mouse's paws, and tag in TW.

DETAILING
Paint the paws on the candy cane with GS. Two coats may be needed. Mix a dark gray by combining GS and LB. With this, detail the ear, face, paws, body, feet, mouth, and whiskers. "Candy stripe" the candy cane in TR and also use that color to outline the tag. Mix TR and TW and use the mixture to paint in the ear and nose. Complete the detail with an eye of LB and a final stripe of TW down the middle of the candy cane.

FINISHING
Glue all pieces together, but do not put on the bow. Spray and, when the spray is dry, glue on the bow and add "To Cat" to the tag using a permanent marker. Drill a 1/16" hole in the top, and string with metallic thread for hanging.

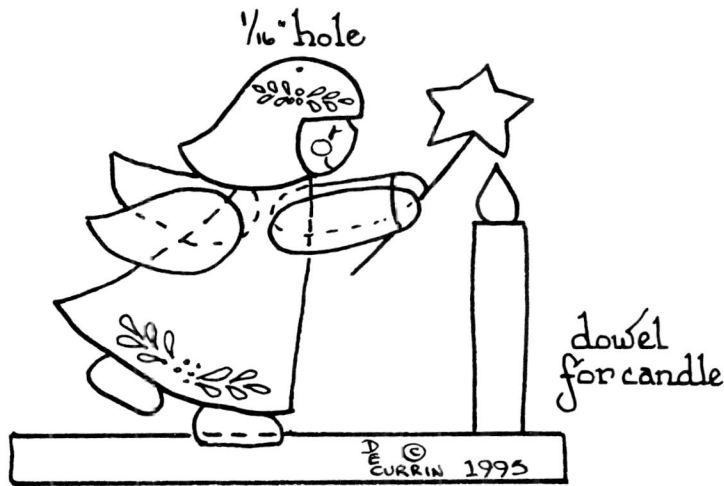

21. ANGEL LIGHTING CANDLE (Photo on p. 32)

8 Pattern Pieces: 1 body, 2 arms, 2 wings, 1 flame, 1 star, 1 base (dowel rod candle is described below)

PALETTE
AG Antique Gold
DR Dusty Rose
FG Forest Green
FT Flesh Tone
LB Lamp Black
TR True Red
TW Titanium White

ADDITIONAL SUPPLIES
Toothpick for wand
Dowel rod, 1/4" diameter (for candle)

PRELIMINARY PAINTING
Follow the General Directions for transferring, cutting, and basecoating. Start by painting the dress TR; head (including hair section), hands and feet FT; candle FG; star and candle flame AG; and wand stem and base LB.

DETAILING
Paint hair in using AG. Add face detail by painting eye and mouth LB and cheeks DR. Lighten AG with TW and outline star and add marks to flame. The decorative detail on the dress and halo are made by pollywog brush strokes of FG (see Worksheet #1, page 8). On the halo add dots of TR; dress dots are TW.

FINISHING
Glue all pieces together using a really strong glue, such as superglue, and spray. Drill a 1/16" hole in the top of the angel's head and string with metallic thread for hanging.

Worksheet #3

Angel Faces

When doing angel faces always keep features delicate.

1. Basecoat with flesh color
2. Add eyes, mouth and nose with Black.
3. Paint cheeks on. For more delicate cheeks lighten the color with flesh.
4. Add hair; remember all angels are not blonde! Hair may also be short.
5. Outline hair with darkened shade of hair color.

Santa Face #1

1. Basecoat hat brim, beard/mustache, and face area all white
2. Paint in face (allow for hair and mustache) Add eyes in Black.
3. Finish detailing by outlining pom pom, cuff, beard/mustache, and hair in gray; add nose and mouth.

Worksheet #4

Santa Face #2

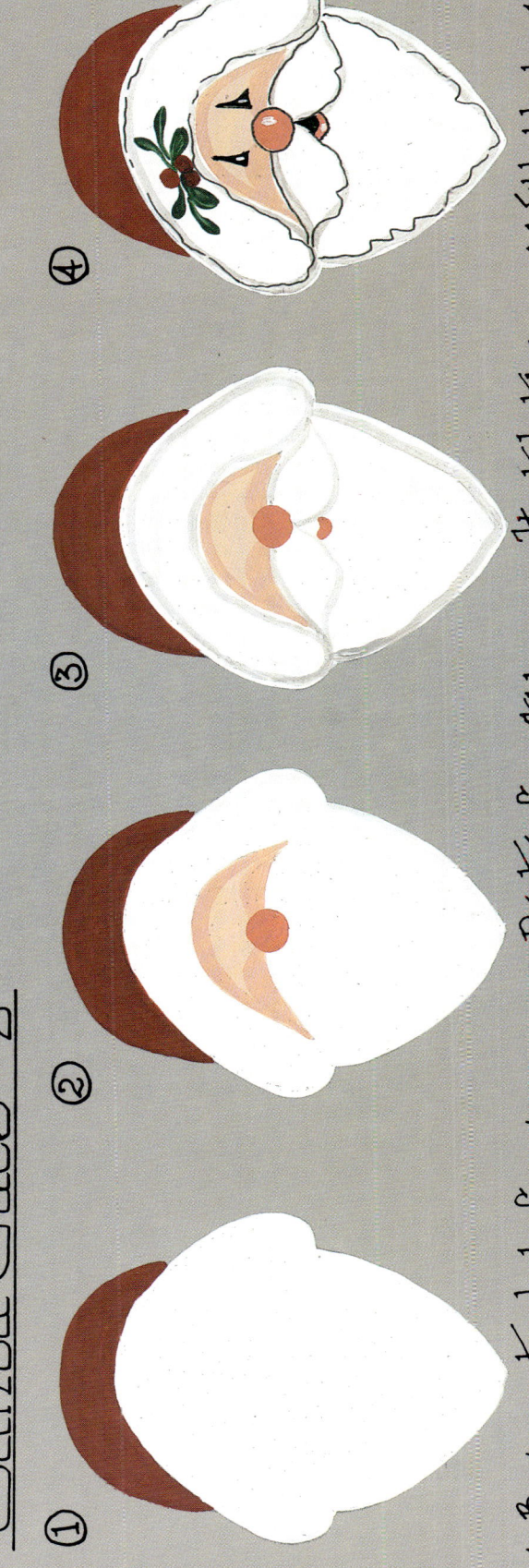

1. Basecoat whole face, space and hat brim; mustache/beard with white.

2. Paint in face. Add cheeks and under hat accent (a mix of 3T, 1R, 1Row 1R). Darken the cheek mix for nose.

3. Float hat brim mustache/beard with BS. Add lip.

4. With black add eyes, mouth and outline. Paint white accent on nose; lip. Finish with leaves and berries.

Santa Face #3

1. Basecoat face with flesh.
   A. Using a very small stencil brush and "wispy" strokes basecoat the beard and mustache with charcoal.
   B. Go over beard and mustache with GS; allow charcoal to show through.

2. Place a third layer over the beard and mustache using white. (a #0 round brush is used for mustache) With black add eyes; mouth. Cheeks are painted in. (see SantaFace #2 for colors) and also nose and lip. Dab on hat brim; finish with leaves and berries.

22. HEART AND HOLLY (Photo on p. 32)

2 Pattern Pieces: 1 heart with extensions for gluing, 1 holly/berries

PALETTE
CR   Country Red
FG   Forest Green
LB   Lamp Black
TR   True Red
TW   Titanium White

PRELIMINARY PAINTING
Follow the General Directions for transferring, cutting, and basecoating. Start by painting the heart and berries TR, and the holly leaves FG.

DETAILING
Float the edge of the heart with a wide band of CR and let dry. Over this add a very fine line of LB. To detail the holly leaves and the berries (see Worksheet #1, page 8). The single snowflake is painted in TW. Although the wording can be painted on in LB before the ornament is sprayed, it is much easier to do the wording with a permanent marker after spraying.

FINISHING
Glue the two pieces together and spray. Drill a 1/16" hole in the middle of the berries and string with metallic thread for hanging.

23. GINGERBREAD COUPLE

3 Pattern Pieces: 2 hearts, 1 gingerbread couple

PALETTE
DC   Dark Chocolate
FG   Forest Green
LB   Lamp Black
SB   Sable Brown
TR   True Red
TW   Titanium White

PRELIMINARY PAINTING
Follow the General Directions for transferring, cutting, and basecoating. Start by painting the gingerbread couple SB, and the hearts TR.

DETAILING
Float edges of both gingerbread people with a mixture of SB and DC. Top this with a fine line of LB. Add eyes, noses, and mouths in LB. The neck details are slightly different for each gingerbread person. The man has a holly leaf tie painted in FG and detailed in lightened FG (mix FG and TW) with TR dots. The woman has a FG bow highlighted with lightened FG, and TR dots. Paint a TW "stitch" line around both hearts and the appropriate words/date.

FINISHING
Glue all pieces together and spray. Drill a 1/16" hole and string with metallic thread for hanging.

24. PATCHWORK SANTA   (Photo on p. 32)

4 Pattern Pieces: 1 Santa, 1 star, 1 heart, 1 tree

PALETTE
AG   Antique Gold
BS   Burnt Sienna
CR   Country Red
DC   Dark Chocolate
DR   Dusty Rose
FB   French Grey/Blue
FG   Forest Green
FT   Flesh Tone
GS   Grey Sky
LB   Lamp Black
NB   Navy Blue
SB   Sable Brown
TW   Titanium White
WN   Warm Neutral

ADDITIONAL SUPPLIES
19 gauge wire (9" per ornament)
Twine (four 5" pieces per ornament)
26 gauge wire (9" per ornament)

PRELIMINARY PAINTING
Follow the General Directions for transferring, cutting, and basecoating. Start by painting the body and hat WN, head and beard TW, gloves FG, and feet LB. The star is painted AG, heart CR, and the tree FG with a SB base. Don't worry if the colors look bright; an antiquing process will soften them.

DETAILING
Paint the face FT and the cheeks DR. Float the edges of the hat brim, beard, and mustache with GS. Now paint eyes and mouth space in LB. Mix DR and a small amount of CR to make the color for the nose and lower lip (similar to Santa #2 on Worksheet #4, page 25). Paint these in. The really fun part of this Santa is doing the patchwork coat and hat (see Worksheet #2, page 9). Lightly pencil off the coat in sections and, using as much variety as possible with your paint combinations, double plaid each section of the coat and hat. Since it is a lot of detailing, you may opt to do only the plaid on the front of the ornament. If this is what you choose to do, then when you antique the coat and hat, merely antique the back at the same time.

Antique the star, heart, tree, and Santa coat and hat with a piece of paper towel or rag dipped in water, then in a small amount of DC. Be sure to keep away from the face, beard, and hat brim. Finally, spatter paint the star, heart, and tree with TW. Add very fine lines around the hat brim, mustache, and beard with a very fine permanent marker. Outlining the cheeks, and nose is optional. Pollywog leaves of FG and berries of CR (see Worksheet #1, page 8) are detailed on the hat brim. Placing a final highlight of TW on nose, lower lip, and each eye is optional, but really brings the Santa to life!

FINISHING
This is another ornament that does not need to be sprayed. Drill 1/16" holes in the star, heart, tree, and top and bottom of each mitten. Wire the star, heart, and tree together with the #26 gauge wire, then attach them to the mittens through the lower hole. Place #19 gauge hanging wire through the top hole in the mittens. Complete the ornament by tying two pieces of twine on each side of the hanging wire.

BS, FB, and NB were used for the plaid.

25. SIMPLE ANGEL WITH RAFFIA BOW (Photo on p. 32)

4 Pattern Pieces: 1 angel body/head, 1 set wings, 1 set arms, 1 heart

PALETTE
AG Antique Gold
DR Dusty Rose
FB French Grey/Blue
FT Flesh Tone
GW Gooseberry Pink + White
LB Lamp Black
TW Titanium White

ADDITIONAL SUPPLIES
19 gauge wire (10" piece per ornament)
Raffia (approximately eight 18" strands)

PRELIMINARY PAINTING
Follow the General Directions for transferring, cutting, and basecoating. Start by painting the arms, body, and wings TW. Paint the entire head FT and the heart GW.

DETAILING
Paint in the hair with AG. Then add the face using LB for eyes, nose, and mouth and DR for cheeks. The dress is detailed by painting a simple plaid (see Worksheet #2, page 9) of FB, making sure that you leave room for the collar. A double plaid (also on Worksheet #2) in your choice of colors would also be a lovely treatment for the dress. Use GW to add a bow and outline the wings. Complete detailing with a TW "stitching" line around the heart.

FINISHING
Glue the arms and heart to the angel body and spray. Drill a 1/8" hole in the top of both wings and thread with the wire. Be sure to twist the wire to form a loop at the top for hanging. Tie raffia at the top of the wire and allow the tails to hang down.

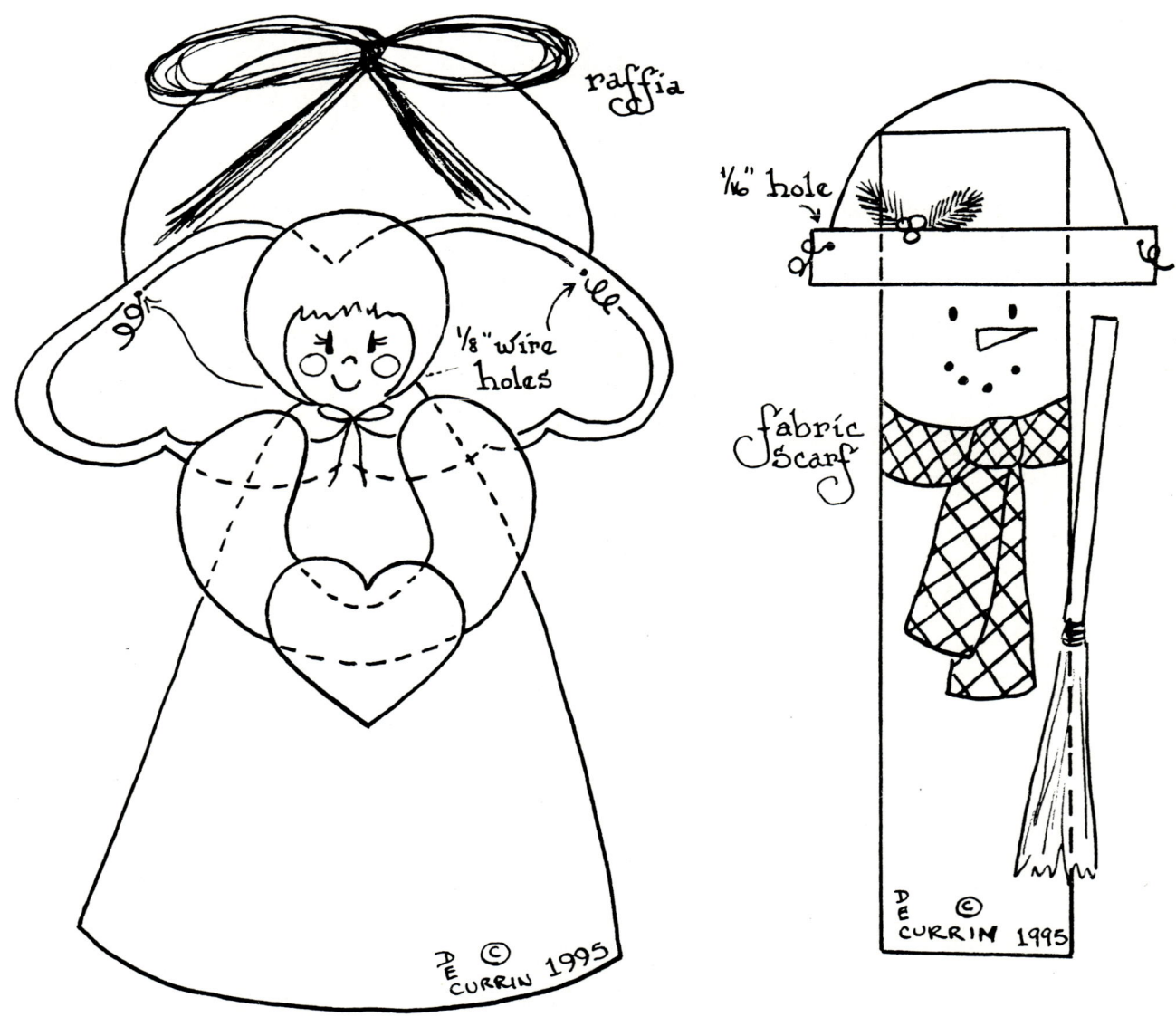

26. FENCE POST SNOWMAN (Photo on back cover)

2 Pattern Pieces: 1 snowman and hat top, 1 hat brim

PALETTE
BS Burnt Sienna
DC Dark Chocolate
LB Lamp Black
TW Titanium White

ADDITIONAL SUPPLIES
Scrap of fabric for scarf
Artificial greens and berries
Mini broom
26 gauge wire

PRELIMINARY PAINTING
Follow the General Directions for transferring, cutting, and basecoating. Start by penciling a line between the hat and face of the snowman. Paint the hat and brim LB, and the front of the body only with a mixture of TW and a very small amount of DC.

DETAILING
Sand the front and sides of the hat, brim, and body. Wipe all pieces with a thinned mixture of DC and water. Mix BS and TW for the cheeks, and use a very small amount of it to blush (see description on page 1) the cheeks. Paint eyes and mouth with LB, nose with BS. Spatter all pieces with TW.

FINISHING
Glue the hat brim to the hat, but do not spray. Drill a 1/16" hole on both sides of the hat brim and attach wire. Tie the fabric scarf around the neck and secure with a dab of glue. Complete the ornament by gluing on the greens, berries, and broom.

27. GIRL ON SANTA'S LAP (Photo on back cover)

7 Pattern Pieces: 1 Santa body/head, 1 chair, 2 chair arms, 2 Santa legs, 1 girl, 1 girl arm (with list made from paper)

PALETTE
AG Antique Gold
BH Blue Haze
CR Country Red
DR Dusty Rose
FG Forest Green
FT Flesh Tone
LB Lamp Black
SB Sable Brown
TR True Red
TW Titanium White

ADDITIONAL SUPPLIES
Scrap of white paper for child's list

PRELIMINARY PAINTING
Follow the General Directions for transferring, cutting, and basecoating. Start by painting the Santa body, arms, legs, and hat TR. The cuffs, pompom, hat brim, beard, and face area are painted a mix of TW and SB. (This makes an "antique" looking white.) The chair and chair arms are painted FG, and mittens a lightened FG (mix FG and TW). Boots are LB. The child's face and hair area are painted FT, shirt AG, pants BH, and shoes SB.

DETAILING
Float edges of Santa's hat, mustache, beard, pompom, and cuffs with a darkened mix of TW and SB. Paint in the face with FT. When that is dry, add cheeks of DR and eyes and mouth opening of LB. Darken DR with a small amount of TR, and paint the nose and lower lip (see Santa #2 on Worksheet #4, page 25). Float edges of Santa's red suit and hat with CR and add a belt of LB to his middle. His mittens are a mix of FG and TW. Santa is finished by adding pollywog leaves and berries (see Worksheet #1, page 8) to his hat. The only detail that is needed on the chair

is to spatter with a mixture of FG and TW. The child can be easily detailed by painting the hair and shoe with SB and adding a bow of TW. The face is completed by painting eyes and mouth LB, and the cheek DR. The pants need to have a simple plaid (see Worksheet #2, page 9) of lightened BH. A final accent of TW may be added to Santa's eyes and nose, but that is optional.

FINISHING
Glue all pieces together and spray. Do not add the "list" until after the spraying is finished. Use a very fine permanent marker to add a line around cuffs, hat brim, pompom, beard, and mustache. Drill a 1/16" hole in the top of Santa's hat and string with metallic thread for hanging.

28. HOUSE WITH TREES (Photo on back cover)

2 Pattern Pieces: 1 house, 1 trees/banner

PALETTE
CR   Country Red
FG   Forest Green
LB   Lamp Black
TW   Titanium White
WN   Warm Neutral

PRELIMINARY PAINTING
Follow the General Directions for transferring, cutting, and basecoating. Start by painting the trees FG, arch lightened FG (mix of FG and TW); house a mix of TW and WN, and the roof LB.

DETAILING
Spatter paint the trees and the arch with TW. Add windows and door in LB, then paint fine lines of the WN/TW mixture (same as used to basecoat the house) across windows, around door, and on roof. To complete windows, paint a fine outline in LB around outer edge. Add a small heart of CR; detail on the heart is the WN/TW mixture. The house becomes a Christmas house when a wreath of lightened FG with CR dots is added to the door. If you do not wish a Christmas house, then do not paint the wreath.

FINISHING
Glue both pieces together and spray. Drill a 1/16" hole in the top of the ornament and string with metallic thread for hanging. You may choose to write the verse on at this time using a permanent marker. Or, you may personalize it or leave it blank.

29. TEDDY IN STOCKING (Photo on back cover)

4 Pattern Pieces: 1 stocking with presents, 1 horn, 1 candy cane, 1 cuff with teddy head

PALETTE
AG Antique Gold
HG Holly Green
LB Lamp Black
SB Sable Brown
TB True Blue
TR True Red
TW Titanium White
WN Warm Neutral

PRELIMINARY PAINTING
Follow the General Directions for transferring, cutting, and basecoating. Start by painting the cuff, toe, and heel of the stocking TW. The stocking is painted TB, horn AG, candy cane TW, bear head SB, and presents in the back TR and HG.

DETAILING
Paint a simple plaid (see Worksheet #2, page 9), then spatter the stocking in TW. Outline toe and heel, and add "stitch" marks in LB. Paint a fine line in TB around the edge of the cuff. Add the bears paws in SB and outline them in LB. Add pollywog leaves (see Worksheet #1, page 8) in HG and dots in TR. The bear's face is detailed by painting a "snout" of WN. Use LB for eyes, nose, mouth, and face outline. Paint candy stripes on the candy cane in TR and highlight it by adding a fine line in TW down the center. Finally detail the horn by outlining it with SB.

FINISHING
Glue all pieces together and spray. Drill a 1/16" hole in the top of the bear's head and string with metallic thread for hanging.

30. SOLDIER (Photo on back cover)

1 Pattern Piece: 1 soldier

PALETTE
CY Cadmium Yellow
DR Dusty Rose
FT Flesh Tone
LB Lamp Black
SB Sable Brown
TB True Blue
TR True Red

PRELIMINARY PAINTING
Follow the General Directions for transferring, cutting, and basecoating. Start by painting head and hands FT, top portion of hat and pants TB, and jacket TR. Shoes are painted LB.

DETAILING
Paint the hair SB, but do not worry about the hat brim. It will be added in LB and cover the hair color. Add detail lines in LB to jacket (to show arms and cuffs) and to pants. The face is completed by painting eyes, nose, and mouth in LB, and cheeks in DR. The small detail on the hat is painted in CY and there are crossbands of CY on the chest.

FINISHING
Spray the ornament and drill a 1/16" hole in the top and string with metallic thread for hanging.